Elbert Hubbard

Little Journeys to the Homes of Famous Women

Madame de Staël

Elbert Hubbard

Little Journeys to the Homes of Famous Women
Madame de Staël

ISBN/EAN: 9783744754262

Printed in Europe, USA, Canada, Australia, Japan

Cover: Foto ©Andreas Hilbeck / pixelio.de

More available books at **www.hansebooks.com**

ɔl. III. No. 7. Ten Cents.   Per Year, One Dollar.

Little Journeys to the Homes of Famous Women by Elbert Hubbard

Madame de Staël

JULY, 1897

New York and London : G. P.
Putnam's Sons   *   *
New Rochelle, N. Y.   The
Knickerbocker Press   *

Little Journeys

SERIES FOR 1897

Little Journeys to the Homes of Famous Women

Described by ELBERT HUBBARD

The above papers, which will form the series of *Little Journeys* for the year 1897, will be issued monthly, beginning in January.

The numbers will be printed uniform in size with the series of 1895 and 1896, but a vellum deckel-edge paper will be used, and each number will have a portrait as frontispiece. The price of the series of 12 numbers for 1897 will be $1.00 per year ; and for single copies 10 cents, postage paid.

The price for sets or for single copies of the series for 1895 and 1896 will remain as before, 50 cents for the set and 5 cents per copy.

Entered at the Post Office, New Rochelle, N. Y.,
as second class matter

Necker de Staël Holstein

Far from gaining assurance in meeting Buona-
parte oftener, he intimidated me daily more
and more. I confusedly felt that no emotion of
the heart could possibly take effect upon him.
He looks upon a human being as a fact or as a
thing, but not as a fellow-creature. He does not
hate any more than he loves ; there is nothing
for him but himself; all other beings are so
many ciphers. The force of his will lies in the
imperturbable calculation of his selfishness.

Reflections.

214

Three Notable Books

BY ROBERT W. CHAMBERS.

The Maker of Moons. Large 12°, gilt top, $1.50.

"Mr. Chambers has an original creative imagination of great power, and has a dramatic faculty which enables him easily and artistically to shape his stories so that there is no lagging of interest . . . he is a master of natural dialogue, a strong picturesque descriptive writer, and the possessor of a keen sense of humor."—*N. Y. Press.*

A King and a Few Dukes. A Romance. *Second Edition.* Large 12°, $1.25.

"No superior fiction has appeared in months. . . . It is a charming love story, attractively told in a way that is essentially Mr. Chambers' own."—*N. Y. Times.*

"A more charming, wholly delightful story, it would be difficult to name in the whole range of English fiction. That is saying much, but not one bit more than the book deserves. . . . The characters are wonderfully well drawn."—*N. Y. World.*

"This latest of Mr. Chambers' stories is written in a very charming manner, and with all the grace and finish that have made the writings of the author so popular during the past."—*Albany Union.*

The Red Republic. A Romance of the Commune. *Fourth Edition.* Large 12°, $1.25.

"With all its rush and excitement there is a solid basis of painstaking and thoughtfulness in 'The Red Republic.' Mr. Chambers is wholly free from self-consciousness; indeed his gifts seem to be little short of genius. Wonderfully vivid and graphic."—*N. Y. Press.*

"Mr. Chambers shows great familiarity with the many dreadful days of 1871, and Mr. Thiers' policy is critically examined. 'The Red Republic' abounds in action."—*N. Y. Times.*

"The book will commend itself not only for its strength and vividness, but for imagination and fancy. . . . Glows with gentle beauty and romance, putting in striking contrast the barbarity of war."—DROCH in *N. Y. Life.*

G. P. PUTNAM'S SONS

NEW YORK AND LONDON

LITTLE JOURNEYS

TO THE HOMES
OF GOOD MEN AND GREAT

SERIES FOR 1895.

Each number treats of recent visits made by Mr. Elbert Hubbard to the homes and haunts of various eminent persons. The subjects for the first twelve numbers are as follows:

1. GEORGE ELIOT. 2. THOMAS CAR-LYLE. 3. JOHN RUSKIN. 4. W. E. GLAD-STONE. 5. J. M. W. TURNER. 6. JONATHAN SWIFT. 7. VICTOR HUGO. 8. WM. WORDS-WORTH. 9. W. M. THACKERAY. 10. CHARLES DICKENS. 11. OLIVER GOLD-SMITH. 12. SHAKESPEARE.

Per number, 5 cents. Per set, 50 cents.

The series of 12 numbers in one volume is illustrated with twelve portraits, some of which are in photogravure. 16mo, printed on deckel-edge paper, cloth bound, gilt tops, $1.75.

"The series is well conceived and excellently sus-tained. The most captious critic could not suggest an improvement. Never was there more satisfactory packing, in more attractive shape, of matter worth at least ten times the money."—*Buffalo Commercial.*

"The series is particularly interesting, and it seems to us that no one could write more delightfully of authors and their homes than does Mr. Hubbard."—*Boston Times.*

"The publishers have succeeded in placing this volume of 'Little Journeys' typographically among the beautiful books of the day. It is a lovely speci-men of the printers' art."—*San Francisco Call.*

G. P. PUTNAM'S SONS

NEW YORK AND LONDON

MADAME DE STAËL.

I.

FATE was very kind to Madame De Staël.

She ran the gamut of life from highest love to direst pain—from rosy dawn to blackest night. Name if you can another woman who touched life at so many points! Home, health, wealth, strength, honors, affection, applause, motherhood, loss, danger, death, defeat, sacrifice, humiliation, illness, banishment, imprisonment, escape. Again comes hope—returning strength, wealth, recognition, fame tempered by opposition, home, a few friends, and kindly death—cool, all-enfolding death.

If Harriet Martineau showed poor judgment in choosing her parents we can lay no such charge to the account of Madame De Staël.

They called her " The Daughter of
Necker," and all through life she de-
lighted in the title. The courtier who
addressed her thus received a sunny
smile and a gentle love tap on his cheek
for pay. A splendid woman is usually
the daughter of her father, just as strong
men have noble mothers.

Jacques Necker was born in Geneva
and went up to the city, like many
another country boy, to make his fortune.
He carried with him to Paris innocence,
health, high hope, and twenty francs in
silver. He found a place as porter or
"trotter" in a bank. Soon they made
him clerk.

A letter came one day from a correspond-
ent asking for a large loan and setting
forth a complex financial scheme in which
the bank was invited to join. M. Vernet,
the head of the establishment, was away
and young Necker took the matter in
hand. He made a detailed statement of
the scheme, computed probable losses,
weighed the pros and cons, and when

the employer returned, the plan, all
worked out, was on his desk, with young
Necker's advice that the loan be made.

"You seem to know all about bank-
ing?" was the sarcastic remark of M.
Vernet.

"I do," was the proud answer.

"You know too much, I'll just put
you back as porter."

The Genevese accepted the reduction
and went back as porter without repining.
A man of small sense would have re-
signed his situation at once, just as men
are ever forsaking Fortune when she is
about to smile; witness Cato committing
suicide on the very eve of success.

There is always a demand for efficient
men, the market is never glutted; the
cities are hungry for them—but the
trouble is few men are efficient.

"It was none of his business!" said
M. Vernet to his partner, trying to ease
conscience with reasons.

"Yes, but see how he accepted the
inevitable!"

"Ah! true, he has two qualities that
are only the property of strong men:
confidence and resignation—I think—I
think I was hasty!"

So young Necker was reinstated and in
six months was cashier ; in three years
a partner.

Not long after, he married Susanna
Curchod, a poor governess. But Mlle.
Curchod was rich in mental endowment:
refined, gentle, spiritual, she was a true
mate to the high-minded Necker. She
was a Swiss too, and if you know how a
young man and a young woman, country
born, in a strange city are attracted to
each other you will better understand
this particular situation.

Some years before, Gibbon had loved
and courted the beautiful Mademoiselle
Curchod in her quiet home in the Jura
Mountains. They became engaged.
Gibbon wrote home, breaking the happy
news to his parents.

" Has the beautiful Curchod of whom

you sing, a large dowry?" enquired the mother.

"She has no dowry! I cannot tell a lie," was the meek answer. The mother came on and extinguished the match in short order.

Gibbon never married. But he frankly tells us all about his love for Susanna Curchod and relates how he visited her, years after, in her splendid Paris home. "She greeted me without embarrassment," says Gibbon, resentfully, "and in the evening Necker left us together in the parlor, bade me good-night, and lighting a candle went off to bed!"

Gibbon, historian and philosopher, was made of common clay (for authors are made of clay) like plain mortals, and he could not quite forgive Madame Necker for not being embarrassed on meeting her former lover, neither could he forgive Necker for not being jealous.

But that only daughter of the Neckers, Germaine, pleased Gibbon—pleased him better than the mother, and Gibbon extended his stay in Paris and called often. "She was a splendid creature," Gibbon relates—"only seventeen, but a woman grown, physically and mentally; not handsome but dazzling, brilliant, emotional, sensitive, daring!"

Gibbon was a bit of a romanticist, as all historians are, and he no doubt thought it would be a fine dénouement to life's play to capture the daughter of his old sweetheart, and avenge himself on fate and the unembarrassed Madame Necker and the unpiqued husband, all at one fell stroke—and she would not be dowerless either. Ha, ha!

But Gibbon forgot that he was past forty, short in stature, and short of breath, and "miles around," as Talleyrand put it.

"I quite like you," said the daring daughter, as the eloquent Gibbon sat by her side at a dinner.

"Why should n't you like me—I came near being your papa!"

"I know, and would I have looked like you?"

"Perhaps."

"What a calamity!"

Even then she possessed that same bubbling wit that was hers years later when she sat at table with D' Alembert. On one side of the great author was Madame Récamier, famous for beauty (and later for a certain "Beauty-Cream"), on the other the daughter of Necker.

"How fortunate!" exclaimed D' Alembert with rapture. "How fortunate! I sit between Wit and Beauty!"

"Yes, and without possessing either," said Wit.

No mistake, the girl's intellect was too speedy even for Gibbon. She fenced all 'round him and over him, and he soon discovered that she was icily gracious to everyone, save her father alone. For him she seemed to outpour all the lavish love of her splendid womanhood. It was unlike the usual calm affection of father and daughter. It was a great and absorbing love, of which even the mother was jealous.

" I can't just exactly make 'em out,"
said Gibbon, and withdrew in good order.

Before Necker was forty he had accu-
mulated a fortune, and retired from business to devote himself to literature and
the polite arts. " I have earned a rest,"
he said, " besides I must have leisure to
educate my daughter."

Men are constantly " retiring " from
business, but someway the expected Ely-
sium of leisure forever eludes us. Necker
had written several good pamphlets and
showed the world that he had ability out-
side of money making. He was ap-
pointed Resident Minister of Geneva at
the Court of France. Soon after he became President of the French East India
Co., because there was no one else with
broad enough reach to fill the place. His
house was the gathering place of many
eminent scholars and statesmen. Necker
was quiet and reserved ; his wife was
coldly brilliant, cultured, dignified, religious. The daughter made good every
deficiency in both.

She was tall, finely formed, but her features were rather heavy, and in repose there was a languor in her manner and a blankness in her face. This seeming dulness marks all great actors, but the heaviness is only on the surface; it often covers a sleeping volcano. On recognizing an acquaintance Germaine Necker's face would be illumined, and her smile would light a room. She could pronounce a man's name so he would be ready to throw himself at her feet, or over a precipice for her. And she made it a rule to know names and to speak them. Then she could listen in a way that complimented, and by a sigh, a nod, an exclamation, bring out the best—such thoughts as a man never knew he had. She made people surprise themselves with their own genius; thus proving that to make a good impression means to make the man pleased with himself. "Any man can be brilliant with her," said a nettled competitor, "but if she wishes, she can sink all women in a room into creeping things."

She knew how to compliment without
flattering; her cordiality warmed like
wine, and her ready wit, repartee, and
ability to thaw all social ice, and lead
conversation along any line, were accom-
plishments which perhaps have never
been equalled. The women who " enter-
tain " often only depress; they are so
glowing that everybody else feels himself
punk. And these people who are too
clever are very numerous ; they seem in-
wardly to fear rivals, and are intent on
working while it is called the day.

Over against these are the celebrities
who sit in a corner and smile knowingly
when they are expected to scintillate.
And the individual who talks too much
at one time is often painfully silent at
another—as if he had made New Year
resolves. But the daughter of Necker
entered into conversation with candor
and abandon ; she gave herself to others,
and knew whether they wished to talk
or listen. On occasion, she could mono-
polize conversation until she seemed

the only person in the room ; but all talent was brighter for the added lustre of her own. This simplicity, this utter frankness, this complete absence of self-consciousness was like the flight of a bird that never doubts its power, simply because it never thinks of it. Yet continual power produces arrogance, and the soul unchecked finally believes in its own omniscience.

Of course such a matrimonial prize as the daughter of Necker was sought for, even fought for. But the women who can see clear through a man, like a Roetgen ray, do not invite soft demonstration. They give passion a chill. Love demands a little illusion ; it must be clothed in mystery. And although we find evidence that many youths stood in the hallways and sighed, the daughter of Necker never saw fit by a nod to bring them to her feet. She was after bigger game—she desired the admiration and approbation of archbishops, cardinals, generals, statesmen, great authors.

Germaine Necker had no conception of
what love is. Many women never have.
Had this fine young woman met a man
with intellect as clear, mind as vivid, and
heart as warm as her own, and had he
pierced her through with a wit as strong
and keen as she herself wielded, her pride
would have been broken and she might
have paused. Then they might have
looked into each other's eyes and lost self
there. And had she thus known love it
would have been a complete passion, for
the woman seemed capable of it.

A better pen than mine has written "a
woman's love is a dog's love." The dog
that craves naught else but the presence
of his master, who is faithful to the one
and whines out his life on that master's
grave, waiting for the caress that never
comes and the cheery voice that is never
heard—that's the way a woman loves!
A woman may admire, respect, revere, and
obey, but she does not love until a passion
seizes upon her that has in it the abandon
of Niagara. Do you remember how Nancy

Sykes crawls inch by inch to reach the
hand of Bill, and reaching it, tenderly
caresses the coarse fingers that a moment
before clutched her throat, and dies content? That's the love of woman! The
prophet spoke of something "passing
the love of women," but the prophet was
wrong—there's nothing does.

So Germaine Necker, the gracious, the
kindly, the charming, did not love. How-
ever, she married—married Baron De
Staël, the Swedish Ambassador. He was
thirty-seven, she was twenty. De Staël
was good-looking, polite, educated. He
always smiled at the right time, said
bright things in the right way, kept
silence when he should, and made no
enemies because he agreed with everybody about everything. Stipulations were
made; a long agreement was drawn up;
it was signed by the party of the first
part and duly executed by the party of
the second part ; sealed, witnessed, sworn
to, and the priest was summoned.

It was a happy marriage. The first three

years of married life were the happiest
Madame De Staël ever knew, she said
long afterward.

Possibly there are hasty people who
will imagine they detect tincture of iron
somewhere in these pages: these good people will say, "Gracious me! why not?"
And so I will admit that these respect-
able, well arranged, and carefully planned
marriages are often happy and peaceful.
The couple may "raise" a large family
and slide through life and out of it without a splash. I will also admit that love
does not necessarily imply happiness—
more often 't is a pain, a wild yearning,
and a vague unrest ; a haunting sense of
heart hunger that drives a man into exile repeating abstractedly the name of
"Beatrice! Beatrice!"

And so all the moral I will make now
is simply this : the individual who has
not known an all-absorbing love has not
the spiritual vision that is a passport to
Paradise. He forever yammers between
the worlds, fit neither for heaven nor hell.

II.

NECKER retired from business that he might enjoy peace ; his daughter married for the same reason. It was stipulated that she should never be separated from her father. She who stipulates is lost—so far as love goes, but no matter ! Married women in France are greater lions in society than maidens can possibly hope to be. The marriage certificate serves at once as a license for brilliancy, daring, splendor, and it is also a badge of respectability. The marriage certificate is a document that in all countries is ever taken care of by the woman and never the man. And this document is especially useful in France, as French dames know. Frenchmen are afraid of an unmarried woman—she means danger, damages, a midnight marriage and other

awful things. An unmarried woman in
France cannot hope to be a social leader,
and to be a social leader was the one
ambition of Madame De Staël.

It was called the salon of Madame De
Staël now. Baron De Staël was known
as the husband of Madame De Staël. The
salon of Madame Necker was only a matter of reminiscence. The daughter of
Necker was greater than her father, and,
as for Madame Necker, she was a mere
figure in towering head-dress, point lace
and diamonds. Talleyrand summed up
the case when he said, "She is one of
those dear old things that have to be
tolerated."

Madame De Staël had a taste for literature from early womanhood. She wrote
beautiful little essays and read them aloud
to her company, and her manuscripts had
a circulation like unto her father's bank
notes. She had the faculty of absorbing
beautiful thoughts and sentiments, and
no woman ever expressed them in a more
graceful way. People said she was the

greatest woman author of her day. "You
mean of all time," corrected Diderot.
They called her "the High Priestess of
Letters," "the Minerva of Poetry,"
"Sappho Returned," and all that. Her
commendation meant success and her in-
difference failure. She knew politics too
and her hands were on all wires. Did she
wish to placate a minister, she invited
him to call, and once there he was as
putty in her hands. She skimmed the
surface of all languages, all arts, all history, but best of all she knew the human
heart.

Of course there was a realm of know-
ledge she wist not of—the initiates of
which never ventured within her scope.
She had nothing for them—they kept
away. But the proud, the vain, the am-
bitious, the ennui-ridden, the-people-
who-wish-to-be, and who are ever looking
for the strong man to give them help—
these thronged her parlors.

And when you have named these you
have named all those who are foremost in

commerce, politics, art, education, phil-
anthropy, and religion. The world is
run by second-rate people. The best are
speedily crucified, or else never heard of
until long after they are dead. Madame
De Staël, in 1788, was queen of the people
who ran the world—at least the French
part of it.

But intellectual power like physical
strength endures but for a day. Giants
who have a giant's strength and use it
like a giant must be put down. If you
have intellectual power, hide it !

Do thy daily work in thine own little
way and be content. The personal touch
repels as well as attracts. Thy presence
is a menace—thy existence an affront—
beware ! They are weaving a net for thy
feet and hear you not the echo of ham-
mering, as of men building a scaffold ?

Go read history ! thinkest thou that all
men are mortal save thee alone, and that
what has befallen others cannot happen
to thee ? The Devil has no title to this
property he now promises. Fool ! thou

hast no more claim on Fate than they who have gone before, and what has come to others in like conditions must come to thee. God himself cannot stay it ; it is so written in the stars. Power to lead men ! Pray that thy prayer shall ne'er be granted—'t is to be carried to the topmost pinnacle of Fame's temple tower and there cast headlong upon the stones beneath. Beware ! beware ! !

III.

MADAME DE STAËL was of an intensely religious nature throughout her entire life ; such characters swing between license and ascetism. But the charge of atheism told largely against her even among the so-called liberals, for liberals are often very illiberal. Maria Antoinette gathered her skirts close about her and looked at the "Minerva of Letters" with suspicion in her big open eyes ; cabinet officers forgot her requests to call, and when a famous wit once coolly asked, "Who was that Madame De Staël we used to read about?" people roared with laughter.

Necker, as Minister of Finance, had saved the State from financial ruin ; then been deposed and banished ; then re-called. In September, 1790, he was again

234

compelled to flee. He escaped to Switzerland, disguised as a pedler. The daughter wished to accompany him but this was impossible, for only a week before she had given birth to her first child.

But favor came back and in the mad tumult of the times the freedom and wit and sparkle of her salon became a need to the poets and philosophers, if city wits can be so called.

Society shone as never before. In it was the good nature of the mob. It was no time to sit quietly at home and enjoy a book—men and women must "go somewhere," they must "do something." The women adopted the Greek costume and appeared in simple white robes caught at the shoulders with miniature stilettos. Many men wore crepe on their arms in pretended memory of friends who had been kissed by Madame Guillotine. There was fever in the air, fever in the blood, and the passions held high carnival. In solitude danger depresses all save the very strongest, but the mob (ever the

—

symbol of weakness) is made up of women
—it is an effeminate thing. It laughs
hysterically at death and cries, " on with
the dance." Women represent the oppo-
site poles of virtue.

The fever continues : a "poverty party "
is given by Madame De Staël where men
dress in rags and women wear tattered
gowns that ill conceal their charms.
"We must get used to it," she said and
everybody laughed. Soon men in the
streets wear red night caps, women ap-
pear in night gowns, rich men wear
wooden shoes, and young men in gangs
of twelve parade the avenues at night
carrying heavy clubs, hurrahing for this
or that.

Yes, society in Paris was never so gay.
The salons were crowded and politics
was the theme. When the discussion
waxed too warm someone would start a
hymn and all would chime in until the
contestants were drowned out and in
token of submission joined in the chorus.

But Madame De Staël was very busy

all these days. Her house was filled with refugees, and she ran here and there for passports and pardons, and beseeched ministers and archbishops for interference or assistance or amnesty or succor and all of those things that great men can give or bestow or effect or filch. And when her smiles failed to win the wished-for signature she still had tears that would move a heart of brass.

About this time Baron De Staël fades from our vision, leaving with Madame three children.

"It was never anything but a *mariage de convenance* anyway, what of it!" and Madame bursts into tears and throws herself into Farquar's arms.

"Compose yourself, my dear—you are spoiling my gown," says the Duchesse.

"I stood him as long as I could," continued Madame.

"You mean he stood you as long as he could."

"You naughty thing—why don't you sympathize with me?"

Then both women fall into a laughing fit that is interrupted by the servant who announces Benjamin Constant.

Constant came as near winning the love of Madame De Staël as any man ever did. He was politician, scholar, writer, orator, courtier. But with it all he was a boor, for when he had won the favor of Madame De Staël he wrote a long letter to Madame Charriere with whom he had lived for several years in the greatest intimacy, giving reasons why he had forsaken her and ending with an ecstacy in praise of the Staël.

If a man can do a thing more brutal than to humiliate one woman at the expense of another I do not know it. And without entering any defence for the men who love several women at one time, I wish to make a clear distinction between the men who bully and brutalize women for their own gratification and the men who find their highest pleasure in pleasing women. The latter may not be a paragon, yet as his desire is to give pleasure not corral it, he is a totally different being from the man who deceives, badgers, humiliates, and quarrels with one who cannot defend herself, in order that he may find an excuse for leaving her.

A good many of Constant's speeches were written by Madame De Staël and when they travelled together through Germany he no doubt was a great help to her in preparing the *De l' Allemagne.*

But there was a little man approaching from out the mist of obscurity who was to play an important part in the life of Madame De Staël. He had heard of her wide-reaching influence and such an influence he could not afford to forego— it must be used to further his ends.

Yet the First Consul did not call on her, and she did not call on the First Consul. They played a waiting game. "If he wishes to see me he knows that I am home Thursdays!" she said with a shrug.

"Yes, but a man in his position reverses the usual order, he does not make the first call!"

"Evidently!" said Madame, and the subject dropped with a dull thud.

Word came from somewhere that Baron De Staël was severely ill. The wife was thrown into a tumult of emotion. She must go to him at once—a wife's duty was to her husband first of all. She left everything and, hastening to his bedside, there ministered to him tenderly. But death claimed him.

The widow returned to Paris clothed in deep mourning. Crepe was tied on the door knocker and the salon was closed.

The First Consul sent condolences.

"The First Consul is a joker," said Dannion solemnly and took snuff.

In six weeks the salon was again opened. Not long after, at a dinner, Napoleon and Madame De Staël sat side by side. "Your father was a great man," said Napoleon.

He had gotten in the first compliment when she had planned otherwise. She intended to march her charms in a phalanx upon him, but he would not have it so. Her wit fell flat and her prettiest smile only brought the remark, " If the wind veers north it may rain."

They were rivals—that was the trouble ; France was not big enough for both.

The Madame's book about Germany had been duly announced, puffed, printed. Ten thousand copies were issued and— seized upon by Napoleon's agents and burned.

"The edition is exhausted," cried Madame as she smiled through her tears and searched for her pocket handkerchief.

The trouble with the book was that nowhere in it was Napoleon mentioned. Had Napoleon never noticed the book the author would have been wofully sorry. As it was she was pleased, and when the last guest had gone she and Benjamin Constant laughed, shook hands, and ordered lunch.

But it was not so funny when Fouché called, apologized, coughed, and said the air in Paris was bad.

So Madame De Staël had to go—it was *Ten Years of Exile.* In that book you can read all about it. She retired to Coppet, and all the griefs, persecutions, disappointments, and heart-aches were doubtless softened by the inward thought of the distinction that was hers in being the first woman banished by Napoleon and of being the only woman he thoroughly feared.

When it came Napoleon's turn to go and the departure for Elba was at hand, it will be remembered he bade good-bye personally to those who had served him so faithfully. It was an affecting scene when he kissed his generals and saluted the swarthy grenadiers in the same way. When told of it Madame picked a petal or two from her bouquet and remarked : "You see, my dears, the difference is this, while Judas kissed but one the Little Man kissed forty. . . ."

Napoleon was scarcely out of France before Madame was back in Paris with all her books and wit and beauty. An ovation was given the daughter of Necker such as Paris alone can give.

But Napoleon did not stay at Elba, at least not according to any accounts I have read.

When word came that he was marching upon Paris, Madame hastily packed up her MSS. and started in hot haste for Coppet.

But when the eighty days had passed and the bugaboo was safely on board the *Bellerophon* she came back to the scenes she loved so well and to what for her was the only heaven—Paris.

She has been called a philosopher and a literary light. But she was only socio-literary. Her written philosophy does not represent the things she felt were true—simply those things she thought it would be nice to say. She cultivated literature only that she might shine. Love, wealth, health, husband, children —all were sacrificed that she might lead society and win applause. No one ever feared solitude more ; she must have those about her who would minister to her vanity and upon whom she could shower her wit.   As a type her life is valuable, and in these pages that traverse the entire circle of feminine virtues and foibles she surely must have a place.

In her last illness she was attended daily by those faithful subjects who had all along recognized her sovereignty—in Society she was Queen.   She surely won her heart's desire, for to that bed from which she was no more to rise courtiers came and kneeling kissed her hand and women by the score whom she had befriended paid her the tribute of their tears.

She died in Paris aged fifty-one.

WHEN you are in Switzerland and take the little steamer that plies on Lake Leman from Lausanne to Geneva, you will see on the western shore a tiny village that clings close around a chateau, like little oysters around the parent shell. This is the village of Coppet that you behold, and the central building that seems to be a part of the very landscape is the Chateau de Necker. This was the home of Madame De Staël and the place where so many refugees sought safety. "Coppet is hell in motion," said Napoleon. "The woman who lives there has a petticoat full of arrows that could hit a man were he seated on a rainbow. She combines in her active head and strong heart Rousseau and Mirabeau; and then

shields herself behind a shift and screams
if you approach. To attract attention to
herself she calls, ' Help, help ! ' "

The man who voiced these words was
surely fit rival to the chatelaine of this
vine-covered place of peace that lies
smiling an ironical smile in the sunshine
on yonder hillside.

Coppet bristles with history.

Could Coppet speak it must tell of
Voltaire and Rousseau who had knocked
at its gates ; of John Calvin ; of Mont-
morency ; of Hautville (for whom Victor
Hugo named a chateau) ; of Fanny Bur-
ney and Madame Récamier and Girardin
(pupil of Rousseau) and Lafayette and
hosts of others who are to us but names,
but who in their day were greatest among
all the sons of men.

Chief of all was the great Necker, who
himself planned and built the main edi-
fice that his daughter " might ever call it
home." Little did he know that it would
serve as her prison, and that from here
she would have to steal away in dis-

guise. But yet it was the place she called
home for full two decades. Here she
wrote and wept and laughed and sang:
hating the place when here, loving it
when away. Here she came when De
Staël had died, and here she brought her
children. Here she received the caresses
of Benjamin Constant, and here she won
the love of pale, handsome Rocco, and
here, "when past age," gave birth to
his child. Here and in Paris, in quick
turn, the tragedy and comedy of her life
were played ; and here she sleeps.

In the tourist season there are many
visitors at the chateau. A grave old
soldier, wearing on his breast the Cross
of the Legion of Honor, meets you at
the lodge and conducts you through the
halls, the salon, and library. There are
many family portraits, and mementos
without number, to bring back the past
that is gone forever. Inscribed copies
of books from Goethe and Schiller and
Schlegel and Byron are in the cases, and
on the walls are to be seen pictures of

Necker, Rocco, De Staël, and Albert the first-born son, decapitated in a duel by a swinging stroke from a German sabre on account of a king and two aces held in his sleeve. Beneath the old chateau dances a mountain brook, cold from the Jura ; in the great courtway is a fountain aud fishpond, and all around are flowering plants and stately palms. All is quiet and orderly. No children play, no merry voices call, no glad laughter echoes through these courts. Even the birds have ceased to sing.

The quaint chairs in the parlors are pushed back with precision against the wall, and the funereal silence that reigns supreme seems to say that death yesterday came, and an hour ago all the inmates of the gloomy mansion, save the old soldier, followed the hearse afar and have not yet returned.

We are conducted out through the garden, along gravel walks, across the well-trimmed lawn, and before a high iron gate, walled in on both sides with massive masonry, the old soldier stops, and removes his cap. Standing with heads uncovered, we are told that within rests the dust of Madame De Staël, her parents, her children, and her children's children—four generations in all.

The steamer whistles at the wharf as if to bring us back from dreams and mould and death, and we hasten away, walking needlessly fast, looking back furtively to see if grim spectral shapes are following after. None are seen, but we do not breathe freely until aboard the steamer and two short whistles are heard, and the order is given to cast off.

We push off slowly from the stone pier, and all is safe.

Little Journeys

SERIES FOR 1896

Little Journeys to the Homes of American Authors

The papers below specified, were, with the exception of that contributed by the editor, Mr. Hubbard, originally issued by the late G. P. Putnam, in 1853, in a series entitled *Homes of American Authors.* It is now nearly half a century since this series (which won for itself at the time a very noteworthy prestige) was brought before the public ; and the present publishers feel that no apology is needed in presenting to a new generation of American readers papers of such distinctive biographical interest and literary value.

No. 1, Emerson, by Geo. W. Curtis.
" 2, Bryant, by Caroline M. Kirkland.
" 3, Prescott, by Geo. S. Hillard.
" 4, Lowell, by Charles F. Briggs.
" 5, Simms, by Wm. Cullen Bryant.
" 6, Walt Whitman, by Elbert Hubbard.
" 7, Hawthorne, by Geo. Wm. Curtis.
" 8, Audubon, by Parke Godwin.
" 9, Irving, by H. T. Tuckerman.
" 10, Longfellow, by Geo. Wm. Curtis.
" 11, Everett, by Geo. S. Hillard.
" 12, Bancroft, by Geo. W. Greene.

The above papers form the series of *Little Journeys* for the year 1896, and are printed in the same general style as the series for 1895. Per set, 50 cts. ; single copies, 5 cts. ; postage paid.

" We must confess that we are very much taken by this chaste volume. The illustrations are perfectly delightful. The contents have appeared in pamphlet form, and we have referred to them in words of praise as they have appeared. They were well worth being put in more lasting shape, and we therefore heartily welcome this book."—*N. Y. Observer.*

G. P. PUTNAM'S SONS

27 WEST 23D STREET, NEW YORK

The Legacy:

By Elbert Hubbard: a new two-volume novel. The book has 450 pages of text on Dickinson's rough Deckel Edge paper; photogravure portrait of author and illustrations on Japan paper. Bound in bottle-green chamois, silk lined. Price $3.00, for the two volumes, express paid.

The Roycroft Printing Shop,
East Aurora,
N. Y.

The Hudson Library.

Published bi-monthly. Entered as second-class matter. 16°. Per number, paper, 50 cts.

G. P. PUTNAM'S SONS
NEW YORK AND LONDON

By Anna Fuller.

A Literary Courtship.

Under the Auspices of Pike's Peak. Printed on deckel edged paper, with illustrations. 22nd edition. 12°, gilt top $1.25

"A delightful little love-story. Like her other book it is bright and breezy ; its humor is crisp and the general idea decidedly original. It is just the book to slip into the pocket for a journey, when one does not care for a novel or serious reading."—*Boston Times.*

A Venetian June.

Illustrated by George Sloane. Printed on deckel edged paper. 7th edition. 12°, gilt top $1.25

"*A Venetian June* bespeaks its materials by its title, and very full the little story is of the picturesqueness, the novelty, the beauty, of life in the city of gondolas and gondoliers."—*Literary World.*

A Venetian June and *A Literary Courtship* are also put up as a set in a box. 2 vols.

$2.50

Pratt Portraits.

Sketched in a New England Suburb. 10th edition. 16°, paper, 50 cts. ; cloth $1.00

" The lines the author cuts in her vignette are sharp and clear, but she has, too, not alone the knack of color, but, what is rarer, the gift of humor."—*New York Times.*

Peak and Prairie.

From a Colorado Sketch-Book. 3rd edition. 16°. With a frontispiece by Louis Loeb. $1.00

" We may say that the jaded reader, fagged with the strenuous art of the passing hour, who chances to select this volume to cheer the hours, will throw up his hat for sheer joy at having hit upon a book in which morbidness and self-consciousness are conspicuous, by their absence."—*New York Times.*

G. P. PUTNAM'S SONS

NEW YORK AND LONDON

HEROES OF THE NATIONS

>◇<

A series of biographical studies of the lives and work of certain representative historical characters, about whom havè gathered the great traditions of the Nations to which they belonged, and who have been accepted, in many instances, as types of the several National ideals. Edited by EVELYN ABBOTT, M.A., Fellow of Balliol College, Oxford. The volumes are sold separately.

Cloth extra, full illustrated . . . $1.50
Half leather, uncut edges, gilt top,   1.75

1. **Nelson.** By W. Clark Russell.
2. **Gustavus Adolphus.** By C. R. L. Fletcher.
3. **Pericles.** By Evelyn Abbott.
4. **Theodoric the Goth.** By Thomas Hodgkin.
5. **Sir Philip Sidney.** By H. R. Fox-Bourne.
6. **Julius Cæsar.** By W. Warde Fowler.
7. **Wyclif.** By Lewis Sergeant.
8. **Napoleon.** By W. O'Connor Morris.
9. **Henry of Navarre.** By P. F. Willert.
10. **Cicero.** By J. L. Strachan Davidson.
11. **Henry the Navigator.** By C. R. Beazley.
12. **Abraham Lincoln.** By Noah Brooks.
13. **Julian the Philosopher.** By Alice Gardner.
14. **Louis XIV.** By Arthur Hassall.
15. **Charles XII.** By R. Nisbet Bain.
16. **Lorenzo de' Medici.** By Edward Armstrong.
17. **Jeanne d'Arc.** By Mrs. Oliphant.
18. **Columbus.** By Washington Irving.
19. **Robert the Bruce.** By Sir Herbert Maxwell.
20. **Hannibal.** By W. O'C. Morris.
21. **Ulysses S. Grant.** By W. C. Church.
22. **Robert E. Lee.** By Hy. A. White.

>◇<

G. P. PUTNAM'S SONS, New York and London